The Burgo

by

Julián Pérez López
Sexton-Guide

Translated by

Inlingua School of Languages

Burgos

To my parents

Dionisio y Virginia

PHOTOGRAPHS:

Photo Club
Fede
Cámara
Soldevila
A. y J. L. Gutiérrez
Esperón
García Garrabella
Calafell
Subirats
Royuela
Oronoz
Arribas

5.ª edición: 1974

Con las licencias necesarias

Copyright Julián Pérez López
ISBN 84 - 7138 - 436 - 1
Depósito legal: BU - 480 - 1974

Santiago Rodríguez, S. A.
Molinillo, 11-15 - Burgos (España)

Pulchra et ecora

PRESENTATION

Someone said that the art of saying is not more than the art of thinking and the art of feeling.

What thoughts spring from the love-sick soul, although it has not reached the summit in the culture!

This occurs with the author of these pages. He has fallen in love with the thousand and one filigrees of his Cathedral!

For this reason he is a singer, a ministrel who would always like to be the speaker in the height of his towers, calling the people to contemplate it.

Friendly reader. Take this small book into your hands, read it slowly and your spirit will feel captivated not only for the admiration of this jewel, matchless, but also for the tenderness and love that this sacristan puts in each one of his pages, in which he transmits all the warmth and enthusiasm he feels for the art and beauty.

THE DEAN

Views of Burgos

BURGOS

It is a city founded by Count Diego Porcelos, in 884.
A city decorated with art and history where the traveller
finds unlimited satisfactions by contemplating its rich
and magnificent monuments.

On these pages, friendly reader, I am not going to
do more than point out the principal marvels of its
uncomparable Cathedral to you, which for 22 years I
have been explaining to the tourists. They are the ones
who have induced me to write this book and for them
I am offering myself to do it in order that they might
carry in their hands a memory of the most beautiful
Cathedral in the world.

THE AUTHOR

View from the Cloister

The Cathedrals of Burgos

According to historians, the first one was in Oca, an ancient city 40 kilometers from Burgos, founded by the sons of Túbal. In it, the Apostle Saint James established the Episcopal See.

In the year 714 the Mohammedan invasion destroyed it completely. Oca, a profoundly religious city, woke in the Africans all of their hate and fury.

In 1074 the infantas Urraca and Elvira, sisters of Alfonso VI, moved the See from Oca to Gamonal, 2 km. from Burgos on the road to Vitoria.

In 1081 Alfonso VI gave up the palaces he had inherited from his father Fernando so that the Cathedral could be erected in Burgos.

In 1219 the Bishop Mauricio travelled to Germany to bring back to Spain with him Beatriz de Suabia, future wife of Fernando III. He was impressed by the Gothic cathedrals he saw on his way in France and Germany.

On November 30 of the same year the King's wedding was held, and the townspeople were displeased by the fact that the Cathedral was not large enough to accomodate all invited. This caused the Bishop and the King both to agree that such a city as Burgos, Capital of Castile, deserved a more worthy Cathedral which would give glory to God and be the pride of a faithful and hard-working people.

View of the Cathedral and romanesque spires from the eleventh century

THE CATHEDRAL OF BURGOS

An admirable and glorious work of christian art. It was founded by King Fernando III the Saint and Bishop D. Mauricio. On July 20, 1221 they placed the first stone. Nine years later they celebrated the first mass; and forty years later, they consecrated it. Its works lasted, approximately, about 400 years.

There is not any news of the first architect. It is attributed to the master Enrique, followed by Juan Pérez and Pedro Sánchez.

The Cathedral is dedicated to the mystery of the Ascent of the Virgin to Heaven. It can be seen that Burgos was one of the first cities in the world that dedicated their Cathedrals to this mystery.

Already in the XI century, when the Cid was departing for his exile, upon saying good-bye to Burgos, asked for the protection from the Virgin calling her Glorious Saint Mary. This trial that the old romanic Cathedral, which Alfonso VI ordered to be built, was also dedicated to the Ascent.

This Cathedral was sadly destroyed in order to level the ground and build on top the actual one. Until now there do not exist any other memories than some displayed spires in the cloister, found in the excavations which were made upon installing the heating.

Towers of the Cathedral. (Juan de Colonia)

Principal Façade

All of it is sprinkled with decorating elements. The statues of the Kings D. Fernando III and Alfonso VI and the Bishops D. Mauricio and D. Asterio, old Bishop of Oca are found on the sides of the central door.

It has a large rosette with arabic drawings that form the called seal of Salomon. On top there is a gallery with eight statues attributed to the Castilian kings, from Fernando I to Fernando III.

The façade with its towers belongs to the first stage of its construction (XIII century). The two steeples or spires were built in the XV century by the german Juan de Colonia.

Kings' Gallery

The Illuminated Cathedral

A Monumental torch that lightens up the city in the silence of the night.

On June 29, 1970, at 10:10 P. M. in presence of the Authorities and numerous public, this new illumination was inaugurated composed of 278 reflectors.

The Cathedral doors

There are four. All of them are very artistic, save the main one, which was poorly restored in the eighteenth century and strikes a sour note for the entire exterior of the building.

Further up the high side of the building from the main door is the Crown door. It is from the thirteenth century. Its extraordinary artistic beauty is due to the many delicately worked statues.

Farther along, at the bottom of some stairs, is the Leatherwork door, which seems to be a series of histo-

The Coroneria door. Tympanum (XIII century)

Head of the Cathedral

rical carvings in elegantly decorative plateresque style. It is from the sixteenth century. The work of Francisco de Colonia.

Rounding the Cathedral sanctuary, admiring its magnificence and its ornamentation, we reach the most beautiful of all the doors.

Door of the Sarmental

The Door of the Sarmental

It has an ogival flavour. It is distinguished by its pro-
fusion of its ornaments and the beauty of its images.

The tympanum is considered as one of the most perfect works of gothic structure in Europe. Christ-Doctor
is found inside, dictating his word to the four evange-
lists who are writing on a lectern.

The new statue of Bishop D. Mauricio is in the mul-
lion. done by Félix Alonso of Burgos. The original one,
from the XIII century is found displayed in the cloister.

View from the San Fernando Square

Saint Mary Major (XV Century)
(Patroness of the Cathedral and of the Diocese)

Transept

Interior of the Temple

The Cathedral has 19 chapels, 38 altars, 58 pilars, on which the naves are rested, 33 iron gratings and two of bronze in the transcept, 38 arches in the interior hall with its stone railings. The pavement is marble of Carrara, placed in 1863.

The dimensions of the church are 108 m. from the door of Santa María to the Chapel of the Constable and 61 m. from the Golden Staircase to that of the Sarmental. The height of the central nave is 27 m. and that of the Transcept. 50.

About this Cathedral Teófilo Gautier says: «Although we were to look at it for two whole years we would not see all; it is gigantic like a pyramid and delicate like a feminine jewel, and no one can understand how such filigree can stand up during centuries and centuries...».

As soon as possible we are going to run through those places where the artists and the history have left their deepest prints.

Cloister door

Door of the Cloister and the Chapel of the Visitation

The door Is found at the right entering through the door of the Sarmental. It has an uncomparable merit, done by Gil de Siloe in the XV century. The façade is from the XIII century. In its arquivolls it has small stone images representing Patriarchs and Doctors of the Church.

The Chapel of the Visitation is in front, ordered to be built by Bishop D. Alonso de Cartagena to Juan de Colonia in 1446. The highlight is the tomb of the founder, D. Alonso. Without seeing it, an author says, it is possible to have an idea of its beauty and its grandeur. The prelate seems to encourage the value and humanity. Its miter chasuble, crozier and cuchions are extraordinary beautiful. It is done in alabaster by Gil de Siloe.

Following at the right and passing on top the Chapel of San Juan de Sahagún, we will contemplate for some moments the tomb of the Archbishop D. Manuel de Castro. It is made in alabaster, work of Valeriano and Andrés Martínez, father and son, from Burgos, in 1952.

Tomb of the D. Alonso de Cartagena

Vault of the Chapel of the Presentation

Tomb of Don Gonzalo de Lerma

Chapel of the Presentation

It was built in 1520 by Felipe Vigarny.

Its clearness and architecture makes it one of the main chapels.

The double pendentives that hold up the dome, are artistical, which form a neatly worked star.

In the center of the chapel the tomb of the founder, D. Gonzalo de Lerma, is found. Spitted in alabaster by Felipe Vigarny.

The painting on the altar, by Sabatian del Piombo and the gratings by Cristóbal de Andino of Burgos are very notable.

Before leaving the chapel we look at the dome, its gracefulness and charm.

Painting by
Sebastián de Piombo

Holy Christ of Burgos

Chapel of Santo Cristo

It is a wing of the old cloister. A sacred image on the principal altar with the name Santo Cristo of Burgos 'is worshipped. The tradition tells us that a merciful merchant, Pedro Ruiz de Minguijuán, foud it in the high seas and he brought it to Burgos, entrusting it to the Hermits of San Agustín.

Certain authors tell us that it is made of wood covered with buffalo skin. It has a beard and the hair is as if it has born in the statue itself. The head moves to both sides, and the arms, if they are unnailed, fall as if it were fainting. In the hands it has human nails incrusted in the fingers. Some authors say that a corspe waiting for a cross would not cause another impression than that which causes this Santo Cristo.

Five ostrich eggs, brought from Africa, appear at its feet, a curious offering from a merchant.

The devotion towards this sacred image is profoundly rooted in the soul of Burgos. The miracles and prodigies are attributed to it are unnumerable. In its honor there is a Confraternity: *La Real Hermandad del Santisimo Cristo de Burgos*. Its main holiday is September 14.

Altarpiece of the Chapel of Saint Tecla

Chapel of Saint Tecla

The last one which was done in the Cathedral. Founded in 1734 by Archbishop D. Manuel Samaniego. Built by Alberto Churriguera.

The largest retable is a true paradigm of the churriqueresque style, although inside the Cathedral causes discordant effects for its overdone decoration.

At the end of the chapel there is a baptismal font form the XIII century.

The pulpit is work of the sculptor from Burgos, Fortunato Sotillo.

The gratings are well styled, specially t h e tops where the coat of arms of the founder and that of the Cathedral.

int John the Baptist

Altarpiece of the Chapel of Saint Anne

Santa Ana Chapel

Its architecture is solid and in good taste, quite grandiose but with little light.

At the entrance is the tomb of Archdeacon Fernando Díaz de Fuentepelayo. According to Bosarte, it is the most elegant Gothic sculpture in Burgos. It is attributed to Gil de Siloe.

The main altarpiece is the work of Gil de Siloe, (fifteenth century), and constitutes a marvelous work of art.

In the center are San Joaquín and Santa Ana. Jessé sleeps placidly at their feet. From his breast springs the genealogical tree, and all of the Virgin's ancestors are found climbing its branches. The Virgin herself sits on a flower at the top of the tree with the child in her arms.

In front of the altar is the tomb of the founder, Luis de Acuña. It was done in alabaster by Diego de Siloe. This Bishop had asked in his will that no tomb be made for him because tombs were built for the sake of earthly life and did no good for the soul. Notwithstanding, his friends and family paid for this tomb as thanks for the many deeds and gifts he had offered the Cathedral.

One of these gifts was Santa María la Mayor, the beautiful silver Virgin on the main altar.

The Golden Staircase

Built in 1519 by Diego de Siloe. Renaissance style. It was first used as an access to the temple. Now it serves only as a marvel upon which the monument is placed during Holy Week. A master work of its kind, it was even once copied for the Paris Grand Opera. From here, turning to look at the far end of the Cathedral, the best rose window of the Cathedral (fifteenth century), admirable for its form and color, can be seen.

Famous Artists

We do not know anything about the first one. Among the known Colonias, Juan (german), his son Simon and his grandson Francisco (from Burgos) are worth while highlighting, who worked from 1400 to 1542. Gil and Diego de Siloe, father and son, Juan de Vallejo and the French, Felipe Vigarny were contemporanries of the last two.

The Colonias Juan and Simon and the inspired Gil de Siloe worked with the gothic style; the remainder with the renaissance style.

Now, following our itinery, leaving behind a series of chapels with small importance, we are going towards that of the Constable, where we can admire marvelous works of these immortal artists.

Triptych by
Gerardo David

Afteraltar

Behind the apse, in the apse aisle, five medallions which represent the most important scenes of the Calvario are found. The three central ones are work of Felipe Vigarny (XVI c.); the first and last, of Alonso de los Ríos (XVII c.).

The marvelous façade and the grating of the Chapel of the Constable is in front.

Grille of the Chapel of the Constable. (Cristóbal de Andino, XVI Century)

Interior of the Chapel of the Constable

Chapel of the Constable

Everything in it is admirable, artistical and magestic.

It is work of Simón de Colonia (XV c.). The founders were D. Pedro Fernández de Velasco and his wife D.ª Mencía de Mendoza, Constables of Castille.

The gracefulness of the perforated dome, an eight point star decorated from a complicated tracery which, springing fron an irregular base, finishes in an octogono by means of finely worked vaults.

The grandeur of the Chapel is in the sumptous tomb of the founders. The sculptures are made of Carrara marble and they give the impression that they are in a deep sleep. They are attributed to Juan de Borgoña.

The oldest retable is from the renaissance style, by Felipe Vigarny and Diego de Siloe. In the laterals there are two other retables. The one on the right is gothic by Gil de Siloe; the one on the left, by his son, Diego, is plateresque, and the famous sculpture of Saint Jeronimo is found in it.

In the sacristy, besides a rich treasure, the famous painting of María Magdalena is found, attributed to Leonardo de Vinci.

That of Santiago is at the left upon leaving the chapel by Juan de Vallejo (XVI c.), and a few steps ahead the Main Sacristy, in rocoro style. The famous brazier is found here of which we will speak about in the last page. Now we are going to visit the Cloister and the treasure of the Cathedral.

Vault and tomb of the Constables in their Chapel

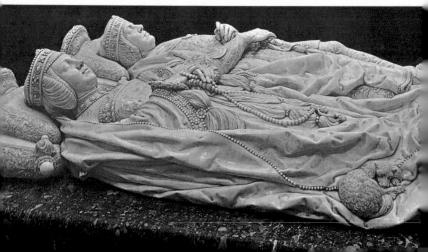

Saint Jerome. (Diego de Siloe)

Jewels of the treasure of the Chapel of the Constable

Mary Magdalene.
(Attributed to Leonardo de Vinci)

43

Cloister

From the thirteenth century. In the form of a perfect square, it is adorned with open arches in ist walls. There are tombs from various centuries, among them the eleventh-century tomb of Mudarra, brought from the monastery of San Pedro de Arlanza in 1896.

In one corner is the silver carriage which carries the gold monstrance in the Corpus procession.

Very close to the carriage are the statues of the King San Fernando —founder of the Cathedral— and his wife Beatriz de Suabia. The King is portrayed in the act of offering her a wedding ring. His romantic and respectful expression, as well as his elegant clothing, is admirable.

Below them is a badly deteriorated small altarpiece from the thirteenth century.

Carriage of silver

Metropolitan Cross (Juan de Arfe)

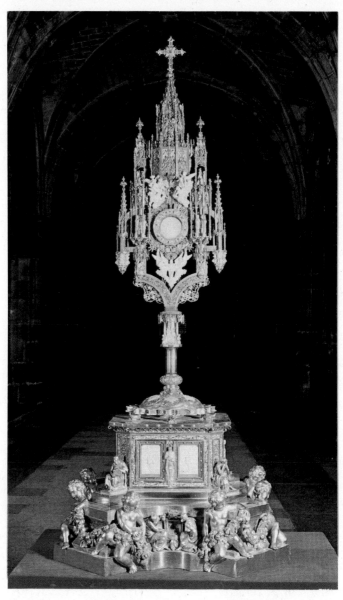

Monstrance of gold (Granda 1927)

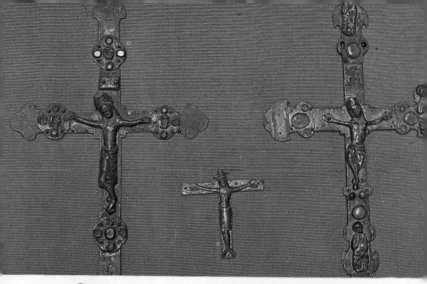

**Romanesque and byzantine crosses
(XI and XII Centuries)**

Reliquary

Amphora (XVII century)

Chapels of the Corpus Christi and Santa Catalina

The first one serves as a pasage to the Capitular Hall. The Coffin of Cid and the Flagellation of Diego de Siloé. The Capitular Hall is admirable for its mudejar caissoned ceiling. A castilian triptych and one of Memling stand out also. The walls are covered with tapestries from the XVI century.

A part of the treasure is kept in the Chapel of Santa Catalina. The great monstrance of Granda (1927) is among the valuable objects as well as, the romanic crosses from the XII c., a byzantine Christ from the XI c. and some beautiful modern chalices of famous goldsmiths of Burgos. Maese Calvo and sons. All the paintings of the Bishops and Archbishops who have directed the diocese are exposed on the walls, and, throughout its ostentatious chest of drawers, interesting documents are exhibited.

Virgin seated (XIII Century)

Pluvial cope.
Arabic style (XIII Century)

Saint John the Baptist Chapel

It is known for its new treasure. The most noteworthy objects are:

A thirteenth-century Moorish cape; a silver golgoltha (fourteenth century); three silver statues of San Pedro, Santiago and San Pablo (fifteenth century); Juan de Arfe's metropolitan Cross; a sixteenth-century choir book; a French Archiepiscopal Cross; a lovely marble Virgin and Child (fifteenth century); two Flemish triptychs; and the bronze, marble and enamel altarpiece from the Granda monstrance.

In the center showcases are rich velvet tunics and rain capes. Tradition has it that some of these capes were used by the Council Fathers during the Council of Basel (fifteenth century).

Bishop's crozier

Ivory Christ (XV century)

Apostle Saint James (XV Century)

Tapestry. Detail (XVI century)

Tapestry

Among the numerous tapestries, four collections stand out. The first one, flemish (XVI c.) represents theological scenes; the second one, also flemish, reproduces scenes of King David; the third, an inferior quality, includes the creation to the death of Abel, and the fourth is formed by seven goblin tapestries that represent the virtues.

Codex' and Manuscripts

The Cathedral possesses great wealth. According to Orcajo, it can be counted among the best of Spain. The oldest documents dates from 774; it is a donation from King. D. Alfonso de Asturias to the church of Valpuesta. The donation of Covarrubias continues in 972, other donations of King D. Sancho to the church of Oca in 1068, and the Letter of the Pledge granted by Cid to D.ª Jimena in 1074, signed by King Alfonso VI and his sisters D.ª Elvira and D.ª Urraca.

A Bible from the IX century and the Complutense also stands out, which the Cardenal Cisneros ordered to be done. It calls attention, as a curious thing, a written letter from Seville, dated Nov. 3, 1571, communicating the defeat of the turkish squad in Lepanto with a plan of how the enemy and christian squads were formed.

Pages of manuscripts

Triptych of the
castilian school

Choir book of (XVI Century)

Flemish Triptych

Paintings

The painting which calls the most attention is María Magdalena, which we already mentioned in the Chapel of the Constable. Although for some authors it is by Leonardo de Vinci, the majority opinion that it is by a disciple of Leonardo de Vinci.

Another notable painting, and which many consider better than the previous one, is the Virgin with the Child, by Memling (XV c.) which is found in the Capitular Hall. It is a work which influences from the first moment of its contemplation.

Painting by Memling (XV Century)

Sculpture

The Cathedral offers one of the richest and finished ensembles since the XIII century. The most admirable sculptures by the critics, after the primitive gothics, are those of the Siloes, the Colonias, Felipe Vigarny, the famous Vallejo and Juan de Ancheta.

The phrases, directed to the greeks, that said: «We build works that any century and any race can understand and which, being human, are eternal», can be applied to these men.

Virgin of ivory (XV Century)

The Scourging. (Diego de Siloe, XVI Century)

The Gold and Silver Work

Our Cathedral, rich in the past centuries, remained very poor in the time of the French invasion.

To-day, among the best jewels that are kept in the treasure, it is necessary to emphasize the monumental Guardian of the Granada goldsmith. All of it is gold, ivory and enamel, weighing 14 kilos; the monstrance is made of platinum and the cross, that finishes it, of precious stones. The ensemble forms a fire-gilding altar step and five displayed compartments that serve as a background, with a great decorative wealth.

The Metropolitain Cross, by Juan de Arfe (XVI c.) is worth while emphasizing, and a beautiful modern chalice, work of the goldsmiths of Burgos already previously mentioned.

Modern Chalice (Maese Calvo)

The Main Chapel

The altar was built by Rodrigo and Martín de la Haya, from Burgos, whose father worked with Francisco de Colonia. It is done in the Renaissance style, composed of three orders: Doric, Ionic and Corinthian. The hollows for the images are very artistic and the statues of the Apostles, with a natural size, admirable for their beauty and energy. The Ascent and the Cross are by Juan de Ancheta. Saint Mary, the eldest, is in the center of the altar, patron of the city. All of it is silver. a gift of Bishop Acuña in the XV c. In the pedestals there are sceneries of the Old Testament. Esther is highlighted in front of King Asuero and Judit killing Holofernes.

The infante D. Juan, son of Alfonso X the Wiseman, is buried at the foot of the altar and beside the Epistle; beside the Evangelio, Count D. Sancho and his wife D.ª Beatriz, daughter of King D. Pedro of Portugal, great grandparents of Fernando the Catholic.

The steps to climb up to the altar are Carrara marble. Six silver candlestick monuments are mounted on them embossed with exquisite works, work of Manuel Crespo, silversmith of Salamanca.

The Chapel is protected by iron gratings (1680) and Bronze ones (1718).

High Altar. Altarpiece (XVI Century)

Choir. (Felipe Vigarny, XVI Century)

The Choir

It has 103 chairs. In each one we could make a particular survey of its labors and works. The chairs are decorated with inlayings of boxtree with fanciful and rare figures, traditions and popular tales. Because of its fantastic details it is an extraordinary work done with so much charm and genius. With reason Amador de los Ríos could say that it is one of the most dignified choirs with admiration of our time.

Its principal author was Felipe Vigarny (XVI c.), Renaissance Style. All of it is carved in walnut. The lying statue is in the center of the founding Bishop of the Cathedral, D. Mauricio carved in wood and covered with a light plate of copper, which af first was spread with stones, disappeared to-day. It comes from the XIII century and it is considered as unique in this class of statues.

It has two parts. That of the epistle was built by Juan de Argueta in 1636; the othe by Juan Manuel de Betolaza and Manuel Cortés, from Burgos, in 1578.

The walnut and mahogany lectern is very notable, coronated by a very beautiful image, by Juan de Ancheta, in 1578.

The grating that closes the choir is magestic, worked by Juan Bautista in the XVI century.

Seated Virgin (by Juan de Ancheta)

Lantern of the Transept. (Juan de Vallejo, XVI Century)

Transept

The most admirable aspect of the Cathedral. Its Plateresque style shows Moorish influence. Below it, the Cid is buried. This marvellous dome serves as his mausoleum. Like a giant canopy open day and night it pays the most glorious homage to Castile's hero.

There are so many days when a mysterious ray of light falls from the transept lantern and lights the golden letters which read: «All are touched by the honor of the one of the opportune birth».

These mortal remains spent 700 years in the San Pedro de Cardeña Monastery. They were brought to Burgos in 1835 to be protected from profanation in the house of the city, as there were few monks remaining in the monastery.

In 1921 the people of Burgos agreed to move them to the Cathedral, it being the most worthy and safest place.

RODERICUS DIDACI CAMPIDOCTOR

MXCIX ANNO VALENTIAE MORTVVS

A TODOS ALCANÇA ONORA

POR EL QUE EN BUEN ORA NACIO

EXIMINA VXOR EIVS

DIDACI COMITIS OVETENSIS FILIA

REGALI GENERE NATA

Tomb of the Cid and D.ª Jimena

Star of the Transcept

Upon seeing it, Felipe II said that it had to be in a box and covered with a slip, in order that, as a precious thing, no one would ever see it except when desired; which seemed to be a work of angels instead of man.

Frankly, it is wonderful to contemplate from the halls the infinity of valuable works of decoration of this eminent Transcept. Among them that which called the most attention, is the coat of arms of Burgos, having as a background the ancient city with its walls, its churches and castle. Here we can say without fear of exaggerating: It looks like a frozen foam.

Between the Transcept and the main altar the b a n n e r which Alfonso VIII carried in the low plains of T o l o s a (1212) hangs there.

Standard of the Navas (XVI century)

The Burgos coat of arms (XVI century)

Triforiums and Stain Glass Windows

One of the most characteristical marks of the Cathedral is the triforium. It is composed of 38 arches, which are decorated on top with beautiful heads of kings, ladies in waiting and knights, etc. It is from the XIII century and decorated in the XV. In the present photograph, below the artistical rosette, two arches of the mentioned triforium appear.

The stain glass windows are from the XIX century. According to Authors the primitive ones were destroyed in the heavy explosion of the Castle by the French in 1813.

The following photograph belongs to a church window on the left part of the nave of the Transcept. It represents the Sermon of the Mountain.

Modern colored stained glass (XX century)

How many styles does the Cathedral have?

This is one of the questions that the tourists frecuently ask me. For this reason, I find myself obligated to make a brief outline about them.

The general appearance of the church belongs to the primitive gothic. The renaissances continues, which appears mixed with the gothic several times, since there are parts where the construction is gothic and the decoration renaissance. The barroque, less frecuent, is plentiful and very overdone in the Chapel of Saint Tecla. The neoclassic is shown in the main door of the Cathedral, in the altar of the Chapel of the Presentation and in the retrochoir. The mudejar style also has its part, specially in the Capitular Hall and in the starred dome of the Transcept. Finally, the rococo appears in the Main Sacristy and in the Chapel of the Relics.

In the present photograph, which corresponds to the apse aisle, we could indicate three of the mentioned styles. The arch on the left is renaissance; the dome, gothic; the decoration of the column, florid gothic, and the medallion on the right, barroque, wit gothic strias.

Apse

The Coffin of Cid

Alfonso VI exiled Cid de Castilla around the year 1081. A narrative poem gathers it together:

«Bitterly cried
the noble Cid with pain,
since they expelled him from Castille
and Castille was his love».

The legend adds: Cid needs money. In colaboration with a good person from Burgos, Martín Antolínez, he filled two chests with stones and sand, presenting them to the jews Rafael and Vidas as a deposit of rich treasures, obtaining with it a loan for 600 gold marks. In the pact it was expressly recorded that the chests would not be oppened for one year; if in this time Cid did not return, the treasures would remain under the power of the Jews. The Poem expresses it in the following way:

«Red the embossed leather, — and thes nails that are very Go for Rchel and Vidas, — bring them quickley;   [gold, for impeding me purchases in Burgos, — and for being exiled
                                                                    [by the King,
my fortune I cannot take; — since it weighs too much;
I will pledge to them — for whatever is just;
and that they take it by night; — so that the christians do not
The Creator sees it — with all his Saints.   [see them,
There is no other way — and I am doing this against my will».

Once Cid conquered Valencia, he returned the loan to the jews, telling them, that although the chests only contained stones and sand, the treasure that was kept inside was his word, more valuable than all the gold loaned. The Narrative Poem of Carolina Michaelis alludes this:

Although what they are taking care of is sand,
that which is in the coffins,
the gold of my truth remained buried inside it.

The Flycatcher

Entering through the main door at the left hand side, there the famous clown is. It dates from the XV century. A special mechanism puts it in combination with the luckt clock which opens and closes the mouth at each stroke of the bell.

I am the Flycatcher
and I am called the Flycatcher;
they gave me this name
five hundred years ago.

From this elevated ogive
I contemplate the crazy people
who run rapidly
in order to see me open the mouth.

But it is not the Flycatcher
who only makes the holiday
also those of you who are, below
and who have the mouth open.

The Brazier

At the entrance of the Main Sacristy, there is a monumental brazier which is lit every day of the year, since the XVII century. A very curious thing for the tourists. In certain occasions, when they remain looking at it, I explain to them as such:

So many look at you, brazier,
without understanding your labor!
Besides giving heat
you are a faithful friend.

You are like a handsome old
who with white hair   [man,
you give us true classes
in the christian meaning.

With your ash dwelling
how you make us think
that the life must end
in dust and nothing.

And in your lit carbon
a reason is reflected:
which as such finishes the heart
consummated little by little.

With what pleasure we look at
                                    [you
and how pleasing is your visit
If everyone, it seems, is invited
to heat their hands.

You have a truefame
you are completely appreciated
and your memory has passed far-
            [ther than the frontier
farther than the frontier.

The tourists- always the same,
asking at the first opportunity,
«What does a brazier sirve for?
in this large Cathedral?

They do not understand your life,
and as such is your slow passing,
days and years without stopping
and with your lit fire.

No one rewards your value,
nor do they hnow that it is your
                                    [mission
to have the carbon just right
in order that the incense catches
                                    [fire.

Look how high your honor is,
because you sirve without being
in order to light the altar   [late
where our Lord is.

CONTENTS